THE BIG LIE

A TRUE STORY

THE BIG LIE

A TRUE STORY

by **Isabella Leitner**

with Irving A. Leitner

Illustrated by Judy Pedersen

SCHOLASTIC INC.

New York

Without the help of my husband,
Irving A. Leitner,
this book would not have been possible.

Copyright © 1992 by Isabella Leitner.
Illustrations copyright © 1992 by Judy Pedersen.
All rights reserved. Published by Scholastic Inc.
SCHOLASTIC HARDCOVER is a registered trademark of Scholastic Inc.

Library of Congress Cataloging-in-Publication Data

Leitner, Isabella.
The big lie: a true story / by Isabella Leitner.
p. cm.
Summary: The author describes her experiences as a survivor of the
Nazi death camp at Auschwitz during World War II.
ISBN 0-590-45569-9
1. Leitner, Isabella — Juvenile literature. 2. Holocaust, Jewish
(1939–1945) — Personal narratives — Juvenile literature. 3. Auschwitz
(Poland: Concentration camp) — Juvenile literature. [1. Leitner,
Isabella. 2. Auschwitz (Poland: Concentration camp)
3. Concentration camps — Poland. 4. Holocaust, Jewish (1939–1945) —
Personal narratives.] I. Title.
D804.3.L45 1992
940.53'18'094386 — dc20
91-40809
CIP
AC

12 11 10 9 8 7 6 5 4 3 2 1   2 3 4 5 6 7/9

Printed in the U.S.A.   37

First Scholastic printing, September 1992

Designed by Marijka Kostiw

*This book is dedicated
to the memory of
my youngest sister, Potyo.
With my love, I am trying
to obliterate the forces
of hate that killed you.*

THE BIG LIE

A TRUE STORY

*This photograph of Isabella
was taken just before
the events described in this book.*

CHAPTER

1

My name is Isabella, and I was born in a small town called Kisvarda.

Kisvarda is located in the northeastern part of Hungary. Today, about nineteen thousand people live there. Of these, only a handful are Jews.

When I lived there, in the 1940s, almost four thousand Jews called Kisvarda home. I was one of them.

I first opened my eyes to the world in Hungary, as did my four sisters and one brother, our parents, their parents, and their parents before them. No one can remember how far back in time our family tree was planted in Hungary, but it is certain that it was a very long time ago.

Today, the date March 20, 1944, might seem like a day in ancient history. Yet to me, it is not very long ago. I can remember the day clearly.

Spring is beginning. Soon the trees will be green again, and flowers will peep out of the earth.

My sister, Potyo, is the "baby" of the family. She has just become a teenager. Then come Regina, Philip, myself, Chicha, and Cipi. All of us are bright, active young people.

We all know that war is raging in Europe, but the fighting is far away from Kisvarda. We know that Nazi Germany has invaded the countries around us. We hear rumors that terrible things have happened — and are still happening — to Jews in those countries.

But what is happening elsewhere cannot happen in our small Hungarian town. Kisvarda is too small, too unimportant, to matter to a great nation like Germany.

This, at least, is what we try to tell each other. But we cannot tell it to my father, because he is in America trying to arrange for our safety.

My father left for the United States in 1939. He left shortly after a band of Hungarian Jew-haters roamed through the streets of Kisvarda looking for Jews to attack. They smashed the windows of Jewish-owned shops. They beat up the shopkeepers and threatened their customers.

"Things will only get worse," my father said. "The Nazis are not yet in Hungary, and already the local Jew-haters are at work.

"We must leave Kisvarda. In America we will be safe. I will send for you when I get immigration papers."

All of us thought he would be gone for a short time, and then we would join him. But we were wrong. For two years my father tried to get papers for us in

America, but all his efforts were in vain. Hungary, Germany's ally, declared war on the United States, and it was too late.

My father is across the ocean, and we are stuck in Kisvarda.

Every day we hear alarming rumors. There is no way for the people of Kisvarda to know whether they are actually true. The Hungarian government controls all the news. Nothing bad about the Nazis' treatment of Jews is printed in our papers or broadcast over Hungarian radio. All the bad news is brought by strangers traveling through town.

With the dawn of March 20, 1944, all this changed. A loud rapping on our window woke us up.

"Let me in! Let me in! It's me, Sanyi. Let me in!"

Sanyi? Our friend who was studying in

Budapest? What was he doing outside our window in Kisvarda?

"Let me in! Let me in, please!"

Inside our house, the words tumbled out of Sanyi's mouth.

"The Germans invaded Budapest yesterday! A whole army of them. They seized the radio station and the newspaper. They're hunting Jews all over the city. I was in the school library when they came. Nazis with guns rushed in.

" 'All Jews come forward!' they shouted. 'All Jews stand up! *Los! Schnell!* Come forward! Fast!'

"They shoved books and papers about. They dragged kids out of their seats. They overturned tables and chairs. They scattered books all over the floor.

"Students were screaming. Boys and girls were crying. Kids were trying to hide.

"In the confusion, I escaped through an open window. I made my way to the railroad station and took the night train to Kisvarda.

"For the whole three hundred kilometers, I was scared to death. I'm still shaking with fear.

"Please hide me until sunset. I'll be gone after dark."

True to his word, Sanyi left that evening for his parents' village.

We never heard from him again.

CHAPTER

2

Overnight, life in Kisvarda changed. What we had previously believed to be only talk now became fact.

The town crier strode into the public square. He was a short man with a peaked cap and a tin drum.

Rat-a-ta-tat! Rat-a-ta-tat! Rat-a-ta-tat!

The town crier beat his drum, and everyone came running.

"Attention! Attention!" the short man cried.

"Here are the orders from Budapest. Listen carefully. The orders must be obeyed.

"1. Starting tomorrow, all Jews must wear a yellow star on their clothes to mark them as Jews.

"2. Starting tonight, no Jew can walk the streets after 7:00 P.M.

"3. Starting tomorrow, no Jewish children can go to public school."

We could not believe our ears. How could the town crier be saying such things? There must be some mistake.

But there was no mistake. Mama sewed yellow stars on our clothes that afternoon. She kept us indoors after 7:00 P.M. And she kept Regina and Potyo home from school the following morning.

Rat-a-ta-tat! Rat-a-ta-tat! Rat-a-ta-tat!

The town crier was back in the square.

"Attention! Attention!" he cried as we gathered around him. "Today's orders are as follows:

"1. No Jew can own a radio. All Jews must turn in their radios at Town Hall. Refusal will bring punishment.

"2. No Jew can ride a bicycle. All Jews must turn in their bicycles at the police station. Refusal will bring punishment.

"3. No Jews can talk to non-Jews in public. These orders will be strictly obeyed!"

As each day passed, new rules were announced. Jews cannot do this. Jews cannot do that.

Passover, the Jewish festival of freedom, was upon us, but we found it hard to celebrate the ancient escape of our ancestors from slavery in Egypt.

Our family was separated, when we should have been together. Father was far away in America, lonely and worried. We were in Hungary, fearful and wearing yellow stars on our clothes.

Our radio was in a closet at Town Hall. We had no music — and, worse — no news about the world. We all felt like prisoners in our own homes in Kisvarda.

The day after Passover, two Hungarian gendarmes came to our home. Unlike our regular police, who carried only sidearms, they carried rifles with fixed bayonets and wore feathered hats.

"Get your family together. Take food and clothing," one of them shouted at Mama. "Take enough, but be outside in ten minutes!"

Terrified, we immediately obeyed — Mama, Cipi, Chicha, Philip, Regina, Potyo, and I.

In the courtyard, other Jewish families were gathering — Mrs. Klein and her handicapped daughter, Esther; Mrs. Fried and her five little children, each of them crying; Mrs. Hirsch, the widow, her niece, and her aged father, all of whom lived together; and Mrs. Feld and her unruly flock of kids.

"Behave yourselves!" Mrs. Feld was screaming at her children. "Behave yourselves! Can't you see what's happening?"

"All right," we heard a shout, "let's go!"

Slowly, the courtyard emptied. We all marched in a ragged line under the gendarmes' watchful eyes.

Mama, Chicha, and I were carrying suitcases bulging with clothing. Philip was carrying blankets and bedding. Cipi and

Regina had an assortment of bags containing food, soap, brushes, pots, and kitchen utensils. And Potyo had her favorite dress and coat draped over her left arm. In her right hand, she clutched a schoolbag filled with books.

Several blocks away, in a vacant rundown area, we met groups of Jews from other neighborhoods. They were already gathered and waiting. For what? We didn't know. We knew only what the armed Hungarians told us. And they told us nothing.

At long last, each family was given quarters in the rundown area. A ghetto was to be formed. In spaces where four or five people once lived, thirty or forty of us were now crowded.

In our cramped space, we dropped our bundles. We were very tired and confused.

"The first thing we do," Mama said, "is clean up. We don't know how long we'll be here, so we must be clean. We mustn't get sick."

Mama unpacked the soap and brushes and went to work. We all helped, hauling water, brushing, and scrubbing. The kitchen floor. The sink. The window. The toilet. The old table and chairs we found there.

All around us, other Jewish families were doing the same thing — cleaning, scrubbing, washing. We were afraid of disease, and we knew that cleanliness would help us to stay healthy.

The gossip was that we would be resettled in the "East" — wherever that was — but, in the meantime, it was important to stay clean.

CHAPTER

3

May twenty-eighth was my birthday, but we had no celebration. That day, a young German soldier came to the ghetto with a gleaming pistol and a barking dog.

"You will all be ready at 4:00 A.M. for deportation," he announced. "Each of you can take along 50 kilos of belongings. Be ready on time, or you will be shot!"

Deportation? What did that mean?

Each of us gathered our best clothes. Dresses. Skirts. Sweaters. Coats. Shoes. Anything and everything we could think of — but only the best, for none of us knew how long the clothing would have to last.

I took my beautiful camel's hair coat, which was too warm to wear at the end of May, but I couldn't leave it behind. I carried it under my arm, together with other precious clothing.

Lastly, we packed whatever food we

had for our journey, just in case — just in case no one would feed us. It wasn't much, but there was bread, jam, and boiled potatoes.

In the dark hour of 4:00 A.M., May 29, 1944, hundreds of families throughout the ghetto began appearing in their court-yards. Each man, woman, and child was carrying a bundle, package, backpack, or suitcase. Each was taking along the best possessions of a lifetime.

A feeling of terror was in the air. There were Nazis with guns and dogs, watching our every move.

Somehow, my brother, Philip, disap-peared.

"Thank God he escaped," my mother whispered.

But moments later, Philip was back. "I couldn't leave without you. We must all go together," he said.

We were herded to the railroad station — our family and all the other Jewish families of Kisvarda.

Main Street was lined with people —
our gentile neighbors. Many of our class-
mates were there, watching as the Nazis
herded us past them. Some of the people
were smiling. They seemed to know they
would never see us again.

At the station, I wondered why the
train had no passenger coaches, only old
cattle cars without windows. The answer
was not long in coming. The Nazis began
to force us into the cattle cars.

The Nazis shouted at us in German, a
language we did not understand. It
sounded like *Los! Los! Los!* It sounded like
dogs barking.

They packed seventy-five to eighty people in each cattle car. Old men and

women. Children clinging to their mothers. Infants in their mothers' arms.

Mama held Potyo close to her body. Philip piled our belongings around them as a wall of protection. Cipi, Chicha, Regina, and I held hands to keep from being separated. When the cattle car was stuffed to its limit, the door was sealed.

There were so many people and so little space, no one was able to sit. We could hardly breathe. With a squeal and a rumble, the train began to roll away from Kisvarda.

For two days, we were given no food to eat, no water to drink. We ate only what we had brought for the journey — the bread, jam, and boiled potatoes. The food was not enough, but we made it last by nibbling.

Many people fell ill. Mrs. Klein went crazy. She screamed hour after hour. Mrs.

Fried's little girl, Sarah, died in her arms. Mrs. Hirsch's aged father died shortly after our journey began. But the train did not stop. When it did, on May thirty-first, we were in Poland, at a place called Auschwitz, a place none of us had ever heard of.

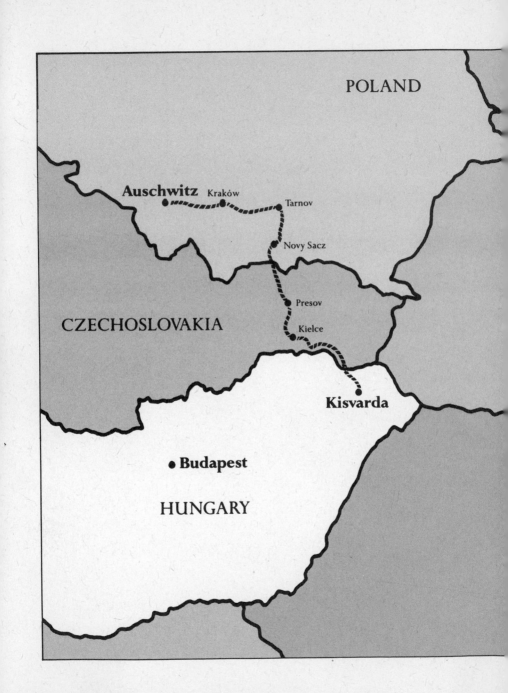

CHAPTER

4

When the cattle car doors were opened, more Nazis with guns and dogs waited for us. Strange-looking men shouted us out of the train. All personal belongings were left behind. My beautiful camel's hair coat, which I had guarded so carefully, was left on the cattle car floor.

"Out! Out! *Los! Los!* Fast! Fast!"

The shouting men were dressed in dirty striped suits, and they carried clubs. They beat anyone who moved too slowly. Later, we found out that they, too, were prisoners of the Nazis. Some were criminals who were working for the Germans.

"Stay with me! Stay together!" Mama shouted at us.

A handsome German officer with a silver pistol was in charge. He wore white gloves, and kept pointing his right thumb either to the left or to the right as each person passed before him. This inspection, we learned, was called "selection." The German officer was Dr. Josef Mengele.

Dr. Mengele sent Mama and my sister Potyo to the left.

"Be strong," Mama cried as she left us. "I love you."

Dr. Mengele sent the rest of us to the right.

"Potyo, I love you!" I shouted, but I don't know whether she heard me.

Philip was led away with the other men who had been sent to the right.

Cipi, Chicha, Regina, and I were taken with the other women to a large, wet room. There, in front of laughing German soldiers, we were forced to take off our clothes for what they called "disinfection."

Standing naked, we were embarrassed, ashamed, and frightened. Then, while we stood there, some women with clippers began to cut off all our hair. Regina and I were crying. Cipi and Chicha were sobbing and trying to hide their nakedness. But the Germans didn't care.

Soon we were totally without hair.

I stared at my sisters. They stared at me. I could hardly recognize them. They no longer looked like Cipi, Chicha, or Regina. They looked like strange two-legged animals that I had never seen before. I was sure that I looked the same to them.

A woman prisoner now threw ragged dresses at us, and we covered ourselves.

Suddenly, amidst all the confusion and unseen by the Nazis, a young man without hair climbed through the window. "It's me, Philip," he whispered. "Eat whatever they give you, because we must

survive. We are prisoners now in Auschwitz, but one day we will be free. And
we will pay them back. So eat and
survive. I love you."

Then he disappeared as swiftly and
mysteriously as he had come.

CHAPTER

5

As the days passed, we learned what Auschwitz was. It was a huge Nazi death camp surrounded by barbed wire fences. The wire was electrified to keep prisoners from escaping. At Auschwitz, between ten and twenty thousand people were killed every day in the summer of 1944.

Much of the killing was done right after the cattle cars arrived with their loads of weary prisoners. Those sent to the left by Dr. Mengele, like Mama and Potyo, were led directly to their deaths.

The killing was done mainly in poison gas chambers that were disguised as shower rooms. The people who were "selected" to die were each given a bar of soap.

"You are going to take a nice hot shower. Remove all your clothes, and leave them where you are. You will find them when you return."

The unsuspecting prisoners, eager to cleanse themselves after their long cattle car journey, obeyed. They did not know they were going to their deaths, for once they were locked in the "shower" rooms, the Nazis released poison gas, not water, into the chambers.

Immediately after the gassing, the dead bodies were hauled to nearby ovens called crematoriums. There, they were burned as fast as possible.

The skies darkened with thick black smoke for miles around, and the smell was awful.

Almost all the prisoners in Auschwitz at this time were Jews. We were kept in barracks called *Blocks*. Each *Block* held one thousand prisoners and one *Kapo*, a prisoner who was in charge. There were thirty-two *Blocks* in my part of Auschwitz. My part was called *Lager C.*

The prisoners in my *Block* had no true beds. Instead, we slept on triple-deck wood shelves called *Pritsches*. I slept on a top shelf, with my three sisters and ten other girls.

The shelf under us also held fourteen girls, and the bottom shelf another fourteen. The shelves often broke, and those on top came tumbling down on the girls below. Screams and shouts filled the night when the *Pritsches* broke. And nobody slept.

Even when the *Pritsches* did not break we could not sleep, because the Germans held roll calls to count us. A roll call was called *Zählappell*, and they were held twice a day.

During *Zählappell*, everyone had to line up outdoors, outside the *Block*. We stood in rows of five, and there were hundreds and hundreds of rows.

Counting us took hours, and during this time, we had to stand without moving. The *Kapos*, who were prisoners themselves, helped the Germans. They beat us if we moved out of line.

The food the Nazis gave us was mostly soup and bread. The soup looked like dirty water and was foul-smelling. The bread, we believed, was made from flour mixed with sawdust. At first, Cipi and Chicha had to hold my nose and force the soup down my throat. Later, because of my hunger, I was glad to get it.

Dr. Mengele decided who was to live and who was to die. If you were sick, old, or frail, you had no chance to live. Young children or mothers with babies were selected to die immediately. Only the strong and healthy could hope to survive.

Everybody was afraid of Dr. Mengele.

Whenever he came to make a selection, Cipi, Chicha, Regina, and I ran from *Block* to *Block* to escape him. One night, he shot at us with his silver pistol. Fortunately, he missed in the dark.

Other times, Dr. Mengele made selections during *Zählappell*. It was impossible to run away then, because we were all standing in rows of five. We stood straight and tall. We pinched Regina's cheeks to make them rosy and healthy-looking. We told her to stand on tiptoe. That way she looked taller than she really was. And Dr. Mengele passed us by.

A few days after we were brought to Auschwitz, some prisoners brought us a piece of wood that had instructions and a message carved into it.

The instructions said: "My four sisters are in *Lager C*. Their name is Katz. Whoever finds this piece of wood, please toss it over the fences until it reaches them."

The message was shorter: "You must live. You simply must. I love you."

Philip had found a way to reach us. His message was brief, but it kept our spirits alive for a long time.

During the six months we spent in Auschwitz, we saw many prisoners starve to death. They starved not because they could not eat the terrible food, but because there was never enough, bad as it was.

The starving prisoners looked like walking skeletons. They were called *Muselmans*. When Dr. Mengele saw a *Muselman*, he sent her off to the ovens.

We saw other prisoners beaten or shot by the Nazis. Once during *Zählappell*, Irma Greza, a woman Nazi officer, made Chicha kneel and hold two rocks in the air until roll call was over.

"You will be very sorry if you drop them," Greza said.

To us this meant that Chicha would be shot.

But Chicha was very brave. She held the rocks high for hours and did not drop them. It was a small victory, but still a victory. Chicha had stayed alive, and that gave all who saw her the courage to carry on.

CHAPTER

6

Late in 1944, Cipi, Chicha, Regina, and I were moved from Auschwitz to another prison, a concentration camp, in eastern Germany. It was called Birnbaumel.

Unlike Auschwitz, Birnbaumel was not a death camp. There were no gas chambers, crematoriums, or electrified barbed wire fences. We slept in hutlike wood barracks called *Celts*.

There were no floors. Each *Celt* rested on the bare earth. Because the walls were very thin, we could hear the wind howling outside.

Every day the Germans marched us out of the camp, through the town, to the edge of a forest. There they forced us to dig holes in the cold, hardened earth. The holes were meant to act as traps for the Russian tanks and trucks, should they advance this far into Germany.

When the Nazi guards looked away, I

stopped digging. Digging, to me, meant helping the Germans. Not digging meant fighting back. And I fought back as often as I could.

December passed, and now it was January 1945. Snow and ice covered the ground. Our spirits were low. We were cold and hungry. I was sick with a high fever. But we were still alive, we were still together, and we were no longer in Auschwitz. That gave us hope.

At the end of the third week of the new year, the Germans decided to move us again. This time, however, there were no trains. The Nazis lined us up in rows of five and began to march us farther inside Germany to Bergen-Belsen, another concentration camp.

It did not matter that many prisoners were too weak to walk for three weeks on the snow-covered roads. The Nazis

beat those who could not go fast enough. When they fell, the Nazis shot them. The journey soon became a death march.

On the third day, a blizzard began. The snow fell heavily, and the wind howled. The column of weary prisoners was much shorter than it had been when we started out. Many prisoners had fallen by the wayside.

As we approached a new village, the Nazi guards alongside us began running to the rear. Some prisoners were trying to escape.

Quickly, Chicha left the column and ran toward what looked like a deserted house off the road. Regina followed Chicha, and I followed Regina. None of us looked back. We all thought Cipi was behind us.

Regina and I crawled into an empty doghouse and hid. We peeped out, but

could see nothing. Chicha, we thought, must be in the house together with Cipi, but we were not sure.

We heard gunshots. Then we saw one of the Nazi guards returning with his dog. We were sure he had killed the girls who had fled.

We looked at each other. Why had we run? Why had we tried to escape? On the march, we were still alive. Now we were risking death. We were certain the guard was going to shoot us.

We crawled out and hid behind the doghouse, terribly afraid. We prayed that the guard's dog would not sniff us.

The guard came closer. Closer. Closer.

We held our breath.

We dared not budge.

The guard and his dog passed. A moment later, they were gone. The wind was blowing away from us, and the dog had not smelled our scent.

When the marching prisoners were out of sight, Regina and I ran to the house. Inside, we found Chicha eating a frozen cabbage.

"Where's Cipi?" she asked.

"She must be in the next house," I replied.

"Here, have some cabbage," Chicha said.

We thought it was the best food we had ever tasted. We searched the pantry and found other food — a smoked pig, smoked meats, sausages. Soon the three of us had bellyaches from overeating. But we didn't mind. We had not eaten so much in a very long time.

All at once, the wintry silence was broken. We heard the sounds of trucks and tanks outside. The Germans have come back to find us, we thought. Now we would all be killed.

In great fear, we peeped out the window. Trucks, tanks, horses, and soldiers were streaming along the road.

But something was different. We had never seen so much equipment. We had never seen the kind of uniforms the soldiers were wearing. Then we spotted their flag.

It was a red flag. And it was fluttering in the wind.

"My God!" we cried. "It's the Russian flag! It's the Russian army!"

With cries of joy, we rushed across the snow to greet our liberators. We knew why the Germans were in such a hurry. They were running in defeat.

Now, at long last, we were free!

CHAPTER

7

We never did find Cipi. We learned later that she also had tried to escape when we did, but the Germans caught her. They beat her with their rifle butts, then forced her to march with the other prisoners to Bergen-Belsen, where she died.

After our liberation, we discovered we were in the village of Jagadschutz in eastern Germany, not far from Breslau, where fighting between the Russians and the Germans was taking place.

Our Russian liberators let us stay in the deserted house, our refuge, where we had been hiding. They fed us, but they also made us work. We had to wash their bloody shirts and take care of a herd of cows.

As the days passed, liberated prisoners began to stream past our house. They were heading toward a train that was supposed to pass through a town called Oelsk. Nobody knew where the town was, but everybody hoped to find it.

We watched the flow from our refuge — Poles, Italians, Czechs, Romanians, Hungarians — people from many different nations. They were on the move, but we didn't want to join them. All we wanted was to eat and rest, to rest and eat. But after six weeks our Russian protectors urged us to go.

"We are running out of food. You must leave. You must go home."

But we didn't want to go back to Kisvarda. That was where we had been forced from home. Finally, we had no choice. We had to leave. We loaded a small wagon with clothing we had acquired since our liberation and, pulling the wagon, joined the host of wanderers on the road.

For the next two weeks, Chicha, Regina, and I trudged along with liberated Jews and freed soldier prisoners — Poles, Englishmen, Frenchmen, Americans, and others. We walked by day wherever the road took us, and slept by night in whatever abandoned homes we found.

At last, we came to a large intersection, where we halted abruptly. Our weariness vanished. Our hearts beat rapidly.

Before us, shining brightly in the sunlight, lay two rows of railroad tracks. And clearly, where there were railroad tracks, there must also be a train.

We abandoned our wagon and, with quickened pace, followed the tracks to a railroad station. Incredibly, we had found the town of Oelsk. We had discovered the gateway out of Germany!

The last time we had been on a train, we had ridden in cattle cars. Now, on the train leaving Oelsk, we were riding in regular passenger coaches. We had embarked on another long journey, but this time, there was room to sit, room to stand, and room to sleep.

In addition, there were lots of Russian soldiers to protect us. Even better, there was a very stout woman soldier of the Russian army who was constantly cooking food to feed us and her comrades.

Where was the train going? We didn't know, and we didn't care, so long as it was rolling away from the land of our Nazi torturers.

In fact, the train was going to Odessa, a bombed-out city on the Black Sea.

After two contented weeks on the train, which chugged and chugged and stopped repeatedly, Chicha, Regina, and I arrived at Odessa. It was April 4, 1945, and the war was still raging.

Everyone got off the train and, together with all the other passengers, we were taken to a large building not far from the railroad. The building was filled with people who, it seemed, were speaking all the languages of the world. Everyone was eager for information. Everyone was asking the same kinds of questions.

"Where are you from?"

"Where are you going?"

"Are you Polish?"

"Are you Hungarian?"

"Are you Italian?"

"Were you in Auschwitz?"

"Have you seen my brother?"

"Have you seen my sister?"

We made friends with a young British flier who had been liberated from a

German prisoner-of-war camp. He was Jewish, and we were able to speak to him in Yiddish.

"We have a father in America. We want to join him. We were in Auschwitz. We lost our mother and two sisters. We lost our brother. We want to go to America."

The young flier took us to an American military official who listened carefully to our story. We could see that he was very moved.

"I will try to help you," the man said in a comforting voice.

Two days later, on April sixth, Chicha, Regina, and I, dressed in khaki military uniforms, sailed for the United States on the liberty ship SS *Brand Whitlock*.

On May 8, 1945, the fighting in Europe ended. Nazi Germany had lost the war, and freedom was triumphant.

On that very day, we arrived in America. Our father met us in Baltimore, Maryland. He hugged and kissed us, and we all cried. It was a happy-sad reunion. We had not seen each other since 1939, six long years ago, when he had sailed for America to try to save his family.

So much had happened since then. We hardly knew what to say.

The following day, our father took us to his home in Brooklyn, New York.

Not long afterward, we received a letter from our brother, Philip. He was alive, but had been shot in the leg by a Nazi. He was recovering in an American hospital in Germany and would be joining us soon.

We were ready to start life anew in America.

AFTERWORD

Hitory calls the years 1939 to 1945 the time of World War II. During these years, the armed forces of Nazi Germany, under the leadership of the dictator Adolf Hitler, brought death and destruction to most of the countries of Europe, the Balkans, and large parts of the Soviet Union.

Hitler and his Nazi party came to power in Germany shortly after the Great Depression began in 1929. Millions of working people around the world lost their jobs. By 1932, almost three million were out of work in Great Britain, twelve million in the United States, and more than five and a half million in Germany.

In 1933, more than 62 million people lived in Germany. Of those, only a half million were Jews. Hitler, a vicious Jew-hater, unjustly accused the Jewish people of causing all the unemployment.

He knew that was not true, but he also knew that the Jews were just a small part of the German population without much political power. He believed that if he repeated the false accusation against the Jews often enough, many non-Jews would believe it. This was known as the "Method of the Big Lie."

Before long, large numbers of unemployed Germans backed Hitler for political office. They were discontented and looking for people to blame for their hardship. They were more than willing to believe Hitler's "Big Lie."

In 1933, President Paul von Hindenburg named the Nazi Adolf Hitler chancellor of Germany. Soon afterward, he became known as *der Führer*, the leader, for he took on the powers of a dictator.

Under Hitler's rule, all labor unions were banned, and all opposition political parties were made illegal. By 1935, the Nazis began to send Jews to concentration camps, where they were mistreated and killed.

This was part of a master plan to solve what Hitler called the "Jewish Problem." The master plan was named the "Final Solution." This was a code phrase for the destruction of the entire Jewish people. The destruction of an entire people is called genocide.

Meanwhile, Hitler put many unemployed Germans back to work in military factories and shipyards. They built speedy war planes, heavy tanks, armored vehicles, and naval vessels. Soon Germany had a powerful army, navy, and air force.

Hitler formed a military alliance with Italy and Japan. The three countries — Nazi Germany, Fascist Italy, and Imperial Japan — were called the Axis.

By 1939, Hitler's armed forces had marched unopposed into the Saar River valley, the Rhineland, Austria, and Czechoslovakia. It appeared that Hitler intended to expand Nazi Germany's rule over all of Europe.

This became very clear in the summer of that year, when Hitler and Stalin, the dictator of the Soviet Union, agreed on a pact of nonaggression, vowing not to attack each other's country.

The pact freed Hitler to use his huge army and air force to attack Poland. This he did, on September 1, 1939, with a *Blitzkrieg*, a lightning war, using all the power at his command.

Immediately, Great Britain and France declared war on Nazi Germany, and World War II began.

Hitler broke his nonaggression pact with Stalin in June of 1941, when thousands of German armored columns invaded the Soviet Union. Thus, the country was drawn into the war against Germany.

On December 7, 1941, Japan, Germany's ally in the Far East, launched a sneak attack on the American naval base at Pearl Harbor, Hawaii. As a result, the United States entered the war against the Axis.

The war continued for over three more years. Many great battles were fought — on the land, on the seas, and in the air.

Millions of people were killed and wounded as Hitler's planes, tanks, and rockets destroyed towns, villages, and cities in Poland, France, Great Britain, Yugoslavia, Greece, Romania, the Soviet Union, and other countries.

Almost everywhere, the Nazi forces were victorious. And, everywhere, the

peaceful, unarmed Jews were brutally at-
tacked.

However, by late 1944, the German
armies had suffered great defeats on the
battlefields, their navy had been largely
destroyed, and their air force had lost
control of the skies. The Germans realized
that they were not going to win the war.

But the Nazis believed they could still
win against the Jews. They wanted to
destroy every single Jew in the world.
Indeed, they almost succeeded in Europe,
for by the war's end in 1945, with the
unconditional surrender of the Axis powers, the Nazis had murdered nearly six
million Jewish men, women, and children.

Nazi Germany's war against the Jews
has come to be known as the Holocaust.